Shopping List

90 cm. towelling
1 reel cotton
1 pkt. needles
140 cm fringe
90 cm. ribbon
1 pkt. hooks
elastic
150 cm. lace

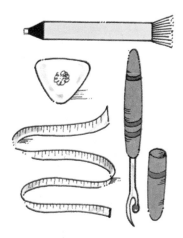
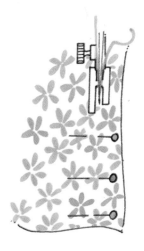

My First 'Show Me How' SEWING BOOK

Written by Jill Wallis
Illustrated by Lindal Mann

PRINTED IN
DEAN & SON Ltd.
52/54 Southwark St.
GREAT BRITAIN
LONDON SE1 1UA
TRADE MARK

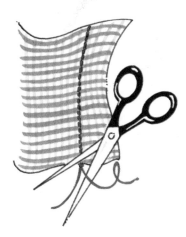

Contents

© Copyright Paul Hamlyn Pty Limited 1973
This edition published by Dean & Son Ltd., 1981
ISBN 0-603-00258-7

Text and illustrations previously published in
My First Sewing Book and *Cooking Knitting Sewing for Girls*

Introduction

While teaching sewing to girls between the ages of 10 and 14, I
realized how keen they were to know more about sewing and try their
hand at a variety of articles. In this book I have compiled articles to
machine and handsew, which are suitable for those who are just
beginners right through to the more experienced sewer.
Most of these articles can be made from scraps left over from
your mother's sewing or some old clothes that you have grown out of and
are allowed to cut up. Perhaps you will be fortunate enough to be able
to buy your own material.
I hope that before you start to make any of the items
you read the instructional section, which will give you the
background knowledge necessary to become a good dressmaker.
I have tested all the patterns and they can be made with the minimum of
expense and time. Many are suitable to use as birthday or Christmas
presents . . . and what could be more personal than a handmade gift!

Jill Wallis

HINTS

Many of the items can be made in a few hours, while others could take almost a day. Do not hurry with any of the patterns. Instead take your time and get perfect results. Most people at some time make mistakes while learning to sew. If you do too, don't worry—just unpick the wrong part and start again.

Safety

1 Keep needles and pins in a tin or pincushion. They could be dangerous if left scattered on chairs or on the floor. (1)
2 Always close your scissors when you put them down. Carry them horizontally, with the points facing toward yourself. (2)
3 Get permission from an adult before starting to use a sewing machine.
4 Do not use the maximum speed of the machine.
5 Keep your hands away from the needle when using the machine. (3)

Cleanliness

1 Before starting to sew, wash your hands thoroughly.
2 Work on a clean table or bench.
3 Keep your sewing in a bag or box. It will collect dust if lying around. (4)
4 Always keep the sewing machine covered when not in use. This will prevent it from getting dusty.

YOUR SEWING BOX

Before you start any sewing you will need to collect some simple tools and sewing materials. Keep them in a box, basket or tin, so that they will always be ready to use. (5) Do not feel that you must go out and buy all these sewing articles. Firstly ask your family and friends if they have any spares they could let you have. In the patterns that follow, this equipment is not listed because it is hoped that you will always have your sewing box beside you.

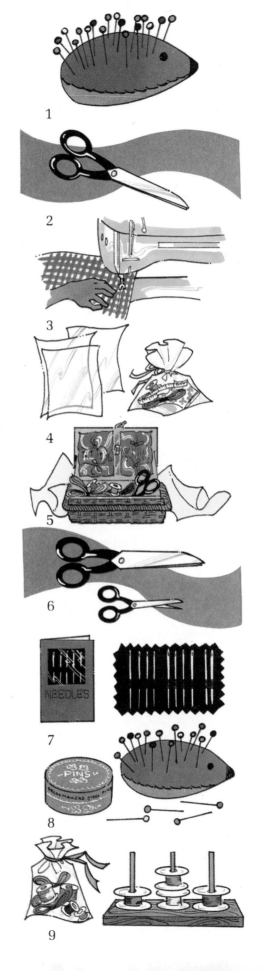

9

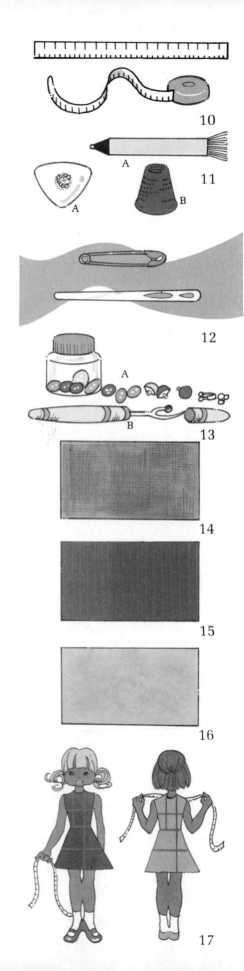

This is a list of the equipment to collect for your basket:

Scissors: A medium-sized sharp pair for cutting out material, and a small pair for cutting threads and button holes. (6)

Needles: A packet of assorted sized needles—from the very fine needles for small stitches to the larger, heavier darning needles for big stitches. (7)

Pins: Some steel dressmaking pins or pins with coloured heads, as these types will not rust. A pin tin or pincushion is essential. (8)

Threads: Collect threads of different colours and thicknesses, including embroidery cottons. Keep all threads in a plastic bag or on a thread stand to prevent them from becoming tangled. (9)

Tape Measure: Try to get a tape marked with metric and imperial measures. A short ruler will also be handy. (10)

Tailor's Chalk: For drawing any necessary markings on the material. (11A)

Thimble: It is essential that you have a close-fitting thimble for hand sewing. (11B)

Safety Pin or Bodkin: For threading elastic. (12)

Buttons, Hooks and Eyes, Press Studs: Collect assorted colours and sizes of each and keep them in a jar or tin. (13A)

Unpicker: For snipping through stitches and unpicking mistakes in your sewing. The unpicker has a sharp point and must be used with care. The top must always be put back after use. (13B)

ALL ABOUT MATERIALS

It is fun to look at the clothes in shops and pick out those you like. But when it comes to buying them, you will usually find that they are very expensive. Often it is more fun making your own clothes because you can choose the exact design, material and colour that you want...and the garments will cost a lot less!

Shopping for Material

Before you go, make a list of:
1 The material you want—colour, design, thickness and yardage.
2 The number of reels of matching thread you will need.
3 Ribbon, elastic, hooks, lace, or any other extras.

Guide to Choosing Materials

There are so many different types of material in the shops that to choose the right one for the garment you are making can be difficult. Here are a few points to help you:

1. There are several thicknesses of fabric. Summer clothes can be made out of cotton or light synthetic fibres. Winter clothes can be made out of woollen fabrics or bulky synthetics.

2. Light-weight fabrics are usually 90 centimetres (36 inches) wide and heavier types are usually 140 centimetres (54 inches) wide.

3. There are three methods of making material:
   Weaving: These fabrics are easy to sew, but will fray if loosely woven. They are the cheapest to buy. (14)
   Knitting: Fabrics made by this method tend to stretch and must therefore be sewn with a very fine stitch. They are usually fairly expensive. (15)
   Bonding: These types of fabric are not strong and become weak after washing, but they are easy to sew. They are moderately priced. (16)

4. Before you make a purchase do not be afraid to ask the shop assistant the following questions:
   - How much does it cost?
   - Can it be washed?
   - Is it difficult to sew?
   - Will it stretch, crease or fray?

MEASURING UP

To get a perfect fit when making clothes for yourself, you must know exactly what your measurements are. Hold the tape measure around or against you firmly, but not tightly. (17)
Write your measurements in the column provided.

	WHERE TO MEASURE	YOUR MEASUREMENTS
Chest	Over fullest part of chest and level around back.	
Waist	Around natural curve of waist.	
Hip	Over widest part of hips.	
Back Bodice Length	From top of shoulder to waist.	
Front Bodice Length	From top of shoulder and over bust to waist.	
Front Length	From top of shoulder to edge of hem.	

11

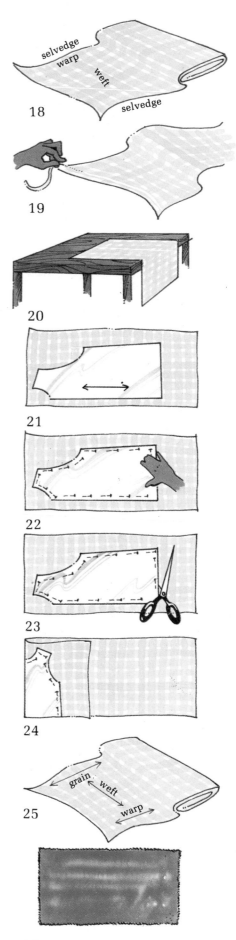

18

19

20

21

22

23

24

25

26

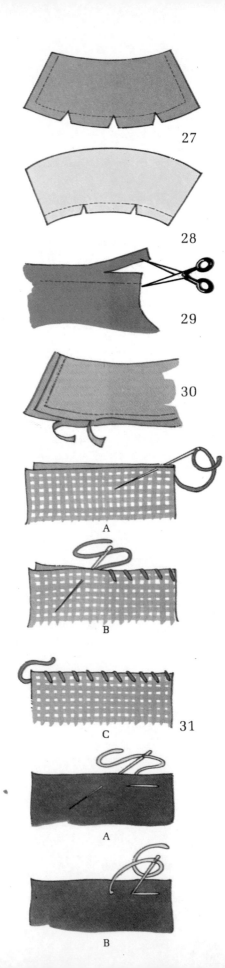

27

28

29

30

A

B

C

31

A

B

CUTTING OUT

Materials are usually folded in half lengthways when you buy them. The woven edges on each side are the selvedges. The threads that run parallel to the selvedges are called the warp threads. The threads that run across are the weft threads. (18)

Guide to Cutting Out

1 Prepare fabric. To do this, straighten one end by pulling a weft thread from across the fabric and cutting along this line to remove excess fabric. (19)
2 Press if necessary, then lay fabric flat on table. Have plenty of room to work on. (20)
3 Place pattern on fabric, making sure the arrow on the pattern is parallel to the selvedges. (21)
4 Pin pattern to fabric, trying not to raise it off the table in the process. (22)
5 Cut with long even strokes, again trying not to raise the pattern and the fabric off the table. (23)
6 To cut two thicknesses of fabric, fold it and place the pattern on top, like this. (24)

DRESSMAKING TERMS

Weft: Threads that run across the fabric. (25)
Warp: Threads that run along the length of the fabric. (25)
Grain: The direction in which the main threads of the fabric run. Also called lengthwise. (25)
Pile: The raised or furry surface of fabrics such as velvet and corduroy. (26)
Seam Allowance: The area between the edge of the fabric and the line of stitching. (27)
Notch: A small 'v' cut into the seam allowance to remove bulk before turning through. (27)
Snip or Clip: A small cut in the raw edge of a seam allowance. (28)
Trim: To cut away extra fabric, as with a seam. (29)
Layer: To trim the seam allowances to different widths to lessen bulk and give a flatter, smoother appearance. (30)

HAND STITCHES YOU WILL NEED TO KNOW

Oversew

This stitch is used to join two pieces of fabric
together or to prevent the edge of a single piece of
fabric from fraying.
A Using a single thread, bring the needle through
   to the right side. (31A)
B Take needle to back and bring through to right
   side again. (31B)
C On single fabric do not pull thread tight or the
   edge will pucker. (31C)

Backstitch

A method of hand stitching two pieces of fabric
together to produce a finished result that resembles
machine stitching.
A Make one stitch, then bring needle to top side
   as illustrated. (32A)
B Fill in the gap by taking one stitch backward. (32B)
C Bring needle to top side and repeat step 2. (32C)

Satin Stitch

This stitch is sewn with embroidery thread to fill
in an outline.
A With tailor's chalk, draw on to garment outline
   of pattern to be satin stitched. (33A)
B Bring needle up at top left hand corner; put in at
   right hand corner. (33B)
C Repeat with stitches parallel. (33C)

Slip Stitch

An invisible hand stitch for finishing hems or
facings and for joining edges of an opening.
A Slip needle up through fold. (34A)
B Pick up two or three threads of the garment
   and slide needle along inside fold. (34B)
C Bring needle out of fold and repeat step 2. (34C)

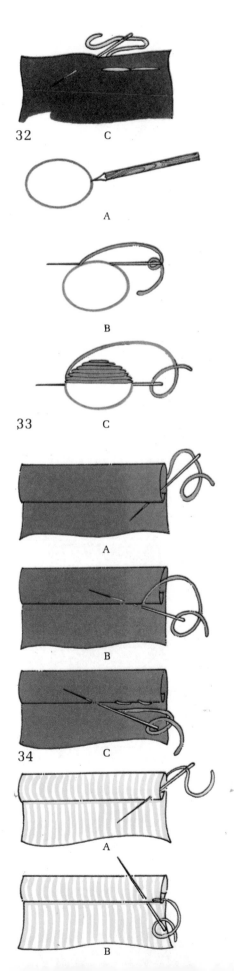

32   C

A

B

33   C

A

B

34   C

A

B

13

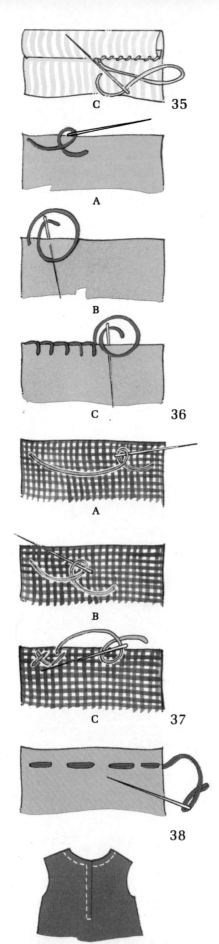

Hemming Stitch

This is a small, firm stitch used to secure one section of a garment to another.
A Slip needle up through fold. (35A)
B Make stitch by putting needle into garment and up through folded edge. (35B)
C Repeat by sewing small stitches close together. (35C)

Blanket Stitch

This stitch is used to join two pieces of fabric together or to give a decorative effect around an edge.
A Bring needle up at left of work. (36A)
B Make loop with thread and bring needle up through material. (36B)
C Repeat along edge of fabric. (Do not pull thread too tight.) (36C)

Herringbone Stitch

This stitch can be used for decoration or to secure a hem edge in place.
A Bring needle to right side of fabric at left-hand corner. (37A)
B Pick up threads above first stitch, pointing needle to the left. (37B)
C Pick up threads in line with first stitch in same way. Repeat steps 1 and 2. (37C)

Tacking

This stitch is used to hold layers of material together. It consists of long, widely-spaced running stitches. Use two thicknesses of a different coloured thread to the colour of the article you are sewing and put a knot at the end. Fasten off with 3 stitches in the shape of a star. (38)

Top Stitching

These are hand sewn stitches made on the outside of a garment. They can be used for decoration at any distance from the edge. (39)

SEWING MACHINES

To make many of the articles you will
need a sewing machine. It can be either a hand
machine or a treadle or electric adults' machine.
You will find it necessary to practise machine
sewing on some scraps of material before you
start work on any garments.

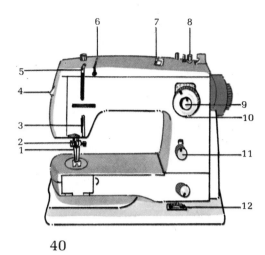

40

These are the parts of a sewing machine (40)
that you should know:
1 Presser-foot
2 Needle-clamp
3 Thread tension
4 Lamp switch
5 Take-up lever
6 Thread tension and thread guide
7 Selector lever for plain or fancy stitches
8 Bobbin winder
9 Left-centre-right adjusting knob (needle
  position)
10 Zigzag adjusting knob
11 Stitch length adjustment (stitch length lever)
12 Fast-Slow Sewing motor control

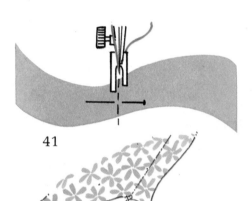

41

42

Before you start work:
1 Read the machine manual carefully.
2 Place the machine on a firm table.
3 Sit at a comfortable height.
4 Work in a good light.
5 Make sure the needle and thread are the right
  thickness for the fabric you are sewing.

Tips for easier sewing:
1 Either remove all pins from the fabric or
  place them diagonally to the stitching line
  then sew over them slowly. (41)
2 Guide the fabric through the machine with
  your left hand.
3 Do not reverse the machine at the end of a line
  of stitching, Tie the threads in a knot, then
  cut them. (42)
4 Wind thread of only one colour on each bobbin.
  (You will, of course, need several bobbins.)(43)
5 Clean the machine often, but use only a
  little oil.(44)

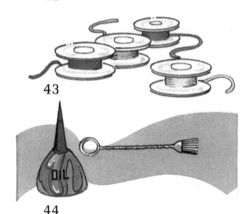

43

44

Pincushion Wristwatch

you will need

tracing paper
pencil
18cm x 9cm (7ins x 3½ins) piece of felt
thread to match felt
kapok or cotton wool for stuffing
felt tipped pen
15cm (6ins) of elastic

STRIP
PATTERN

CIRCLE
PATTERN

instructions

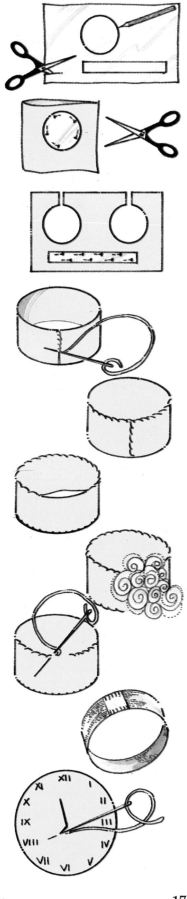

1   Trace outline of circle and strip on to tracing paper. Cut out paper patterns.

2   Fold felt in half and pin circle pattern like this. Cut around circle, through double-thickness of felt.

3   Open out felt and place pattern of strip on it. Cut around pattern. Remove pattern piece.

4   Join ends of the strip with oversew stitches.

5   Oversew the strip to one circle.

6   Join the second circle to the other edge of the strip, leaving 2.5cm (1in) open for stuffing.

7   Push stuffing through opening, making the cushion as fat as possible.

8   Press edges of opening together and oversew neatly.

9   Measure elastic around wrist to get a comfortable fit; join ends. Attach to underside of cushion with hemming stitches.

10   With the felt tipped pen, draw the face of a clock on the top of the cushion and mark in the hands using backstitch.

17

Table Mats
FOR SIX PLACE MATS

you will need

60cm (²/₃yd) furnishing fabric or hessian 140cm (54in) wide
matching embroidery thread

variations

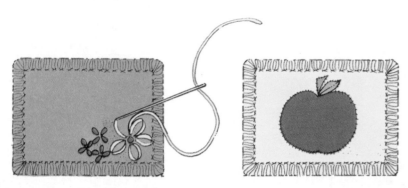

instructions

1 Measure fabric as shown and mark with tailor's chalk. Cut lengthwise into two strips.

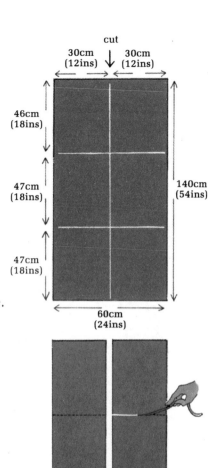

cut

30cm (12ins)

30cm (12ins)

46cm (18ins)

47cm (18ins)

47cm (18ins)

140cm (54ins)

60cm (24ins)

2 Pull a thread out across the marking of each strip of fabric. Cut along the lines made by these threads.

3 Using herringbone stitch, sew around mats, 2.5cm (1in) from the edge.

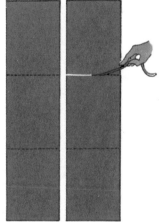

4 When you have completed sewing around mats, fray up to stitches.

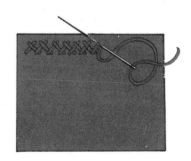

Egg Cosy

you will need

tracing paper
pencil
three 7cm (2½in) square pieces of different coloured felts
glue
embroidery thread

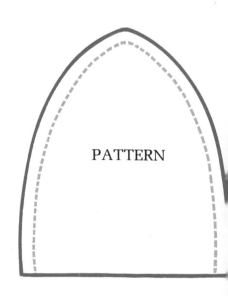

PATTERN

instructions

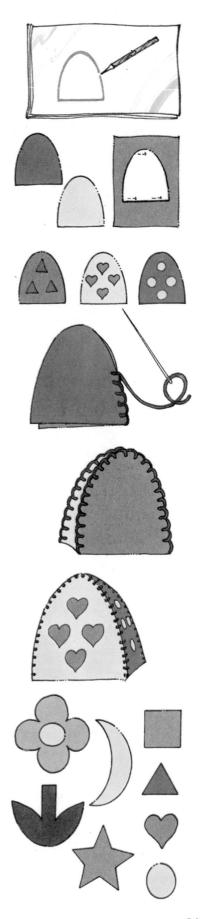

1 Trace pattern on to three thicknesses of tracing paper and cut out.

2 Pin shapes on to the three pieces of felt and cut out.

3 Cut out patterns of your own choice from the felt scraps and glue some on to each shape.

4 With right sides facing each other, blanket stitch two pieces of felt together along one curved side only.

5 Join third piece (right side facing inward) to loose sides, again using blanket stitch.

6 Turn through to right side and gently work seams apart until stitching shows like this.

PATTERN IDEAS

Covered Coat Hanger

you will need

wooden coat hanger
90cm (1yd) of ribbon
cotton wool
thread
15cm x 61cm (6ins x 24ins) length of fabric

variations

instructions

1 Cut 30cm (12ins) length from ribbon; reserve to make bow. Wind remaining ribbon around hook and secure around base.

2 Place cotton wool thickly along both sides of the hanger and wind thread around to hold it in position.

3 Fold material in half over hanger. Fold in 2cm (¾in) hem on all edges and pin together.

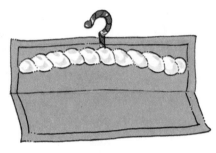

4 Sew small tacking stitches 1cm (½in) from top, using double thread.

5 Gather up so fabric fits length of coathanger.

6 Tie bow at base of hook and hem stitch in place.

Pencil Case

you will need

two 23cm x 15cm (9ins x 6ins) pieces of fabric
20cm (8in) zip
matching thread

variations

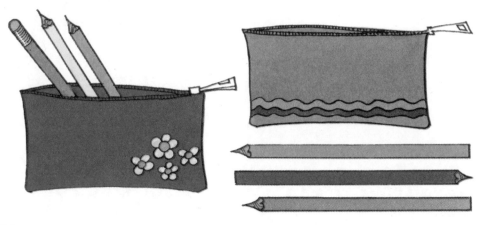

instructions

1 Press 1.5cm (½in) hem on one long side of each piece of fabric.

2 Pin fabric to zip by placing the folded edges together over the teeth. (Allow the pieces to overlap 1.5cm (½in) above and below the zip teeth.)

3 Wrong side up, tack fabric to zip .6cm (¼in) from teeth. Remove pins.

4 Put zip foot on machine and stitch along tacking line.

5 Embroider initials or pattern on to case. To prevent any puckering pin a piece of stiffening to the back before you start.

6 Open zip. Put both pieces of case together, right sides facing. Pin, then tack along the sides and lower edge.

7 Machine along tacking lines and trim edges, as shown. Remove tacking.

8 Turn case to the right side and close zip.

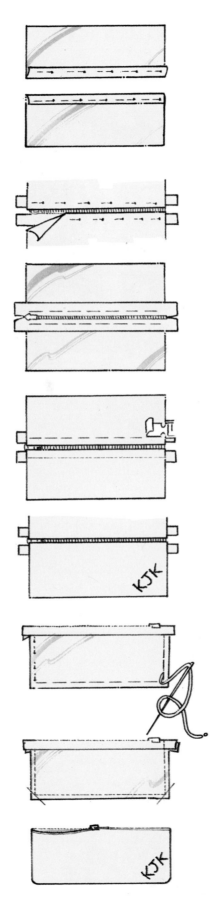

Knitting Needle Tidy

you will need

46cm (½yd) patterned fabric 90cm (36ins) wide
46cm (½yd) plain fabric for lining 90cm (36ins) wide
60cm (²/₃yd) of 2.5cm (1in) wide ribbon

variations

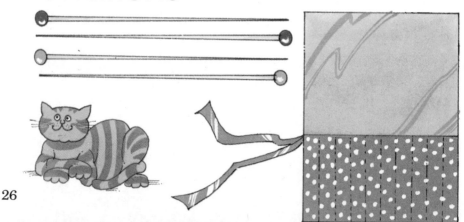

instructions

1 Place fabric right sides together and pin. Machine .6cm (¼in) seams around the sides, leaving 7.5cm (3in) gap to turn through.

2 Trim corners. Turn through to right side.

3 Slip stitch along gap to close opening.

4 Placing right sides together, fold up one end to a depth of 23cm (9ins) to make a pocket. Pin and tack, then machine along both side edges.

5 Turn the tidy right side out and mark the pocket into 14 equal divisions, each approximately 3cm (1¼ins) wide. Tack along divisions.

6 Machine along tacking lines. Tie threads at both ends.

7 Sew two 30cm (12in) lengths of ribbon to one side of the pocket as shown.

8 Fill with needles, roll up, wind ribbon around and tie with a bow.

Skirt

you will need

90cm (1yd) square of cotton fabric
thread to match
tacking thread
76cm (30ins) elastic

variations

instructions

1 Cut fabric in half cross-ways to make back and front of skirt.

2 Put right sides together, pin and tack. Machine a 1.5cm (⅝in) seam along both sides of skirt. Press open with iron.

3 Press under .6cm (¼in) around top edge. Turn under another 3.5cm (1½ins) and pin down. Tack, then machine around folded edge, leaving 1.5cm (½in) gap.

4 Machine around fold again, 1.5cm (½in) above first row of stitching.

5 Measure around your waist and cut elastic 7.5cm (3ins) shorter than measurement. Thread through casing and hand sew ends together.

6 Turn under .6cm (¼in) at bottom edge and machine in place.

7 Turn hem up 5-8cm (2-3ins) according to the length desired. Pin in place, then join using slip stitch.

Midi Top

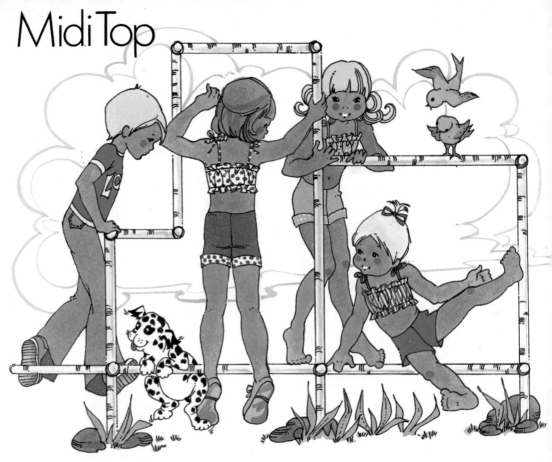

you will need

40cm (14in) length of 90cm (36in) cotton fabric
matching thread
tacking thread
1.4 metres (1½yds) elastic

This top is designed to partner the skirt on the previous page. It is very attractive and will fit busts from 76-92cm (30-36ins) in size.

variations

instructions

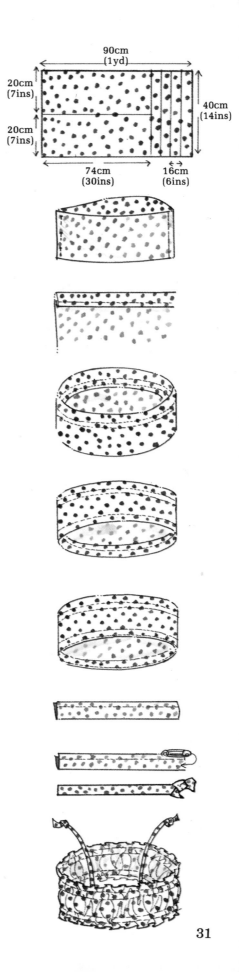

1 Cut fabric as shown in diagram.

2 Place the two large pieces right sides together and pin. Machine a 1.5cm (⅝in) seam down both sides. Press open with iron.

3 Make top casing by turning under .6cm (¼in) then under again another 3.2cm (1¼ins). Pin down and tack, then machine along edge, leaving a 1.5cm (½in) gap at end of stitching to thread elastic through.

4 Machine another row 1.5cm (½in) above first row. This forms the casing and prevents elastic from twisting.

5 Turn bottom edge under .6cm (¼in) then under again another 2cm (¾in). Pin and stitch in place, again leaving a 1.5cm (½in) gap.

6 Machine a row along the edge as indicated in the diagram. This forms the lower elastic casing.

7 Fold each of the 4 strips in half lengthways and machine .6cm (¼in) seam along the lengths.

8 Turn through using a small safety pin or a hair grip. Tie a knot at one end of each strip.

9 Attach other ends to inside of casing in position, approximately 20.5cm (8ins) from each side seam. Hem stitch in place.

10 Measure above and below your bust and cut elastic 7.5cm (3ins) less than those measurements. Thread through casings and oversew together.

31

Headscarf

you will need

46cm (½ yd) fabric
thread to match

variations

instructions

1 Cut fabric as shown in diagram.

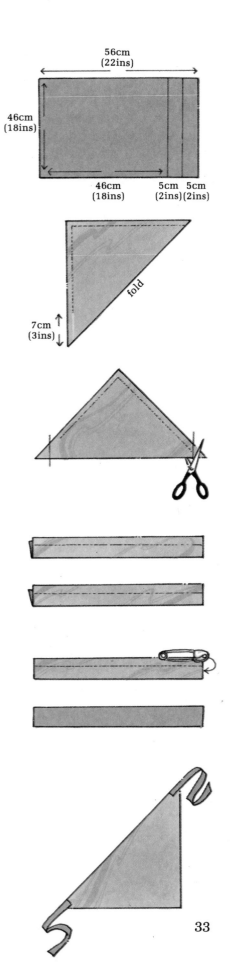

56cm
(22ins)

46cm
(18ins)

46cm
(18ins)   5cm 5cm
          (2ins)(2ins)

2 Fold the 46cm (18ins) square in half diagonally, with right sides facing inward. Machine raw edges together, leaving a 7cm (3ins) gap to turn through.

fold

7cm
(3ins)

3 Trim off corners and turn through. Slip stitch edges of the 7cm (3ins) gap together.

4 Fold strips lengthways, with right sides together. Machine along length leaving a 1:2cm (½in) seam.

5 Using a safety pin, turn through to right side. Push in raw edges of ends and hem stitch to close openings.

6 Hem stitch the ties to scarf.

Apron

you will need

large sheet of paper
pencil
76cm (⁵⁄₆yd) fabric **90cm (36ins) wide**
4.15 metres (4½yds) bias binding
matching thread

variations

instructions

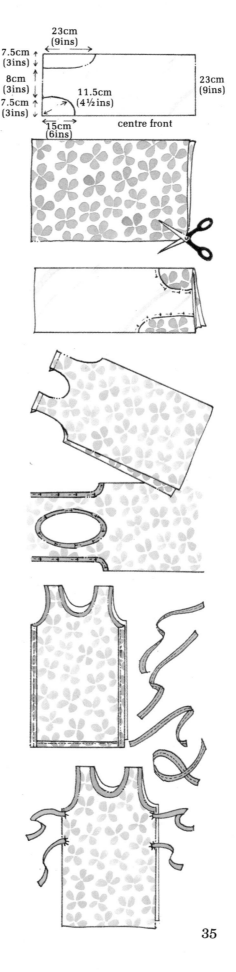

23cm
(9ins)

7.5cm
(3ins)

8cm
(3ins)

7.5cm
(3ins)

11.5cm
(4½ins)

23cm
(9ins)

15cm
(6ins)

centre front

1 Draw a 76cm x 23cm (30ins x 9ins) rectangle on the sheet of paper and carefully mark in the armhole and neckline before cutting around outline of pattern. Mark centre front section of pattern.

2 Fold fabric in half lengthways and cut along folded edge. Fold in half again. There should now be four thicknesses.

3 Place pattern on fabric with centre front edge on the fold. Pin, then cut around armhole and neckline.

4 Remove pattern. Open out two pieces of fabric and join the shoulders with a 1.5cm (½in) seam, as shown. Press seam open with iron.

5 Overlap bias binding around neck and armholes. Pin, tack and carefully machine around edge of bias binding.

6 Press under .6cm (¼in) along sides and across bottom. Turn under another 1.5cm (½in) all around. Pin, tack and machine in place.

7 Cut 8 strips of bias binding, each 23cm (9ins) long. Machine lengthways along centre of each strip to prevent unravelling.

8 Pin a strip on wrong side at base of each armhole and another strip 15cm (6ins) below that. Hem stitch in place.

Poncho

you will need

tracing paper
pencil
90cm (1yd) of 140cm or 150cm
(54in or 60in) wide towelling
3.7 metres (4yds) fringing
61cm (2/3yd) bias binding
matching thread

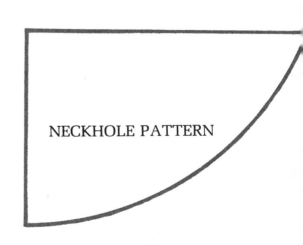

NECKHOLE PATTERN

instructions

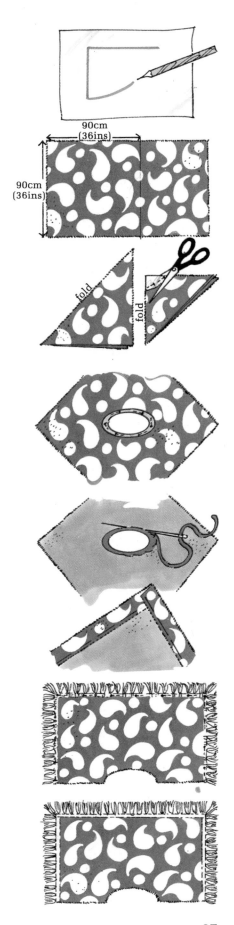

1 Trace pattern of neck hole on to paper and cut out.

2 From the fabric, cut a square with sides 90cm (36ins) in length. (Reserve the left-over strip to make the beach bag on the following page.)

3 Fold the square in half diagonally to form a triangle, and then in half again. There should now be four thicknesses. Place pattern on corner as shown. Pin and cut.

4 Open out bias binding and pin right sides together around neck. Tack then machine .6cm (¼in) from edge.

5 Turn to wrong side and slip stitch down.

6 Turn edges under .6cm (¼in) then under another 1.5cm (½in) to make hem. Tack firmly in place.

7 Cut fringing into four equal lengths and pin to the right side, 1.5cm (½in) in from each edge. Overlap the fringe at each corner and cut off any excess.

8 Machine around the four edges 1.5cm (½in) in and then another row .3cm (⅛in) in. This will hold the fringe flat on the fabric.

Beach Bag

you will need

46cm (½yd) towelling or 46cm (18in) strip
left over from poncho
matching thread
3 metres (3yds) cording

variations

instructions

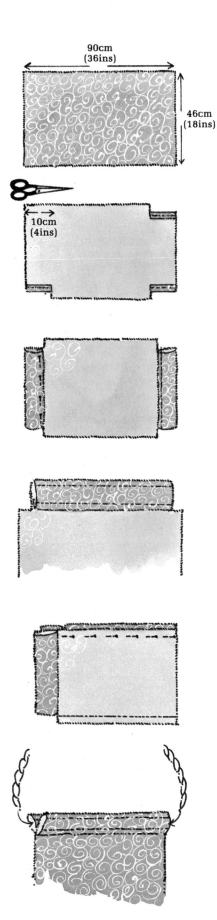

1 Cut fabric to the size shown.

2 Measure 10cm (4ins) from each end and cut in 1.3cm (½in) on each long side, as shown. Turn the 10cm (4ins) flaps to the wrong side and machine in place.

3 To make the cord casing, turn 6cm (2¼ins) back at each end, wrong sides facing. Turn under 1.5cm (½in) of the raw edge. Pin in place, tack, and machine.

4 To complete casing, machine 1.5cm (½in) from the folded edges.

5 Fold material in half, right sides together. Pin, tack, then machine.

6 Turn bag through to right side. Cut cord in half. Thread one length through both casings and tie. From opposite side insert other cord through both casings and tie.

MakeUp Purse

you will need

tracing paper
pencil
30.5cm x 15cm (12ins x 6ins) piece quilted fabric
matching thread
30cm (½yd) bias binding
2 press studs

PURSE FLAP PATTERN

instructions

1 Trace outline of pattern on to tracing paper and cut out.

2 Place pattern on one end of strip, pin and cut out. Put markings A and B on fabric as indicated.

3 Open the bias binding and pin to the right side. Pin to the right side of fabric, starting at A and going around the curved edge to B. Sew .6cm (¼in) in from the edge. Tie both ends of thread.

4 Snip in to A (or the first stitch formed) and to B (or the last stitch formed). Turn bias on to wrong side. Pin, then slip stitch in place.

5 Turn the edge of the other end over .6cm (¼in) and machine along.

6 With right sides together, fold remains of purse in half. Machine along both sides and tie threads at both ends.

7 Snip off corners, being careful not to cut stitching.

8 Turn through. Attach two press studs to hold down flap.

Bob Cap

you will need

tracing paper
pencil
46cm (½yd) wool
or jersey fabric
90cm (36ins) wide
matching thread

CROWN PATTERN

instructions

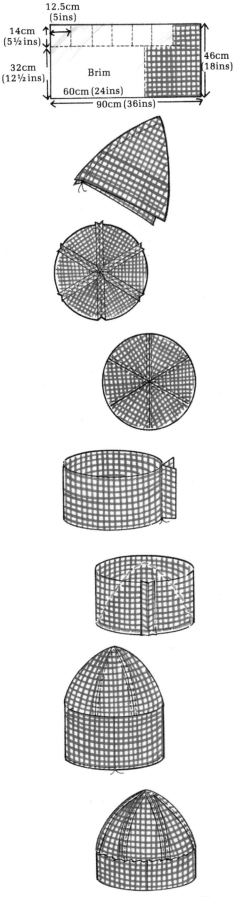

1 Trace pattern of crown on to paper. Cut out the brim and 6 crown pieces as shown.

2 Place two crown pieces together, right sides facing. Pin, tack, then machine along indicated sewing line. Tie threads at ends.

3 Repeat with the other two pairs of crown pieces, then join all the pieces together, as shown.

4 Press all seams open with the iron and top stitch .6cm (¼ in) away from the seam.

5 Fold the brim piece in half and machine 1.5cm (½ in) from the edge. Press seam open.

6 Pin, tack and machine the brim to the crown with right sides together.

7 Press the brim down with the iron. Turn up .6cm (¼ in) along the raw edge and machine.

8 Turn cap inside out, turn up the brim and pin the machine neatened edge to the crown seam line. Tack and then hem stitch in place.

43

Scuffs

you will need

cardboard
pencil
20cm x 25cm (12ins x 12ins) square of leather or felt
tailor's chalk
20cm x 45cm (8ins x 18ins) length of quilting
embroidery thread
1.4 metres (1½yds) bias binding

before you start

Read the instructions carefully and decide on the quality scuffs you
would like to make. Scuffs that will last a lifetime require leather soles,
but those wanted for only a season or two can have felt soles.
If you decide to make leather-soled scuffs, you will have to complete
steps 1 and 2 a few days before you want to make the scuffs.

instructions

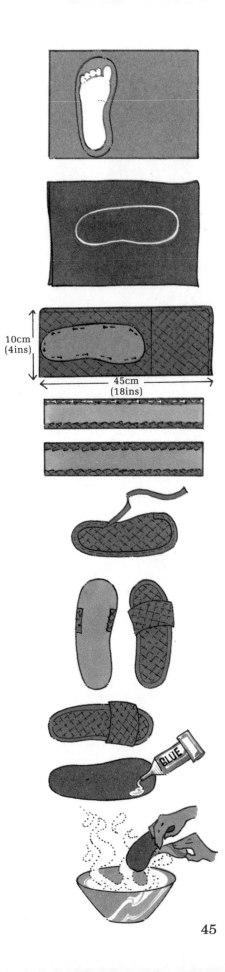

1 Draw an outline of your foot on the cardboard and cut out pattern.

2 If using felt sole, place pattern on double-thickness of felt as shown below, mark outline with tailor's chalk and cut. If using leather sole, take pattern to bootmaker and ask him to cut you a pair of leather or suede soles. Also ask him for a small jar of special shoe glue.

3 Fold the quilting in half lengthways. Place pattern on top, secure, and cut out upper soles, as illustrated. Cut two 20cm x 10cm (8ins x 4ins) strips out of remaining quilting.

4 Turn under a 1.5cm (½in) hem on the long edges of the strips and hem stitch in place on the wrong side.

5 Pin the bias binding over the raw edges of the quilted soles and use small tacking stitches to secure in place.

6 Pin one end of strip under each side of sole, as shown, and hem stitch in place. (Determine the exact position to place the strips to suit your feet.)

7 Put glue on upper side of leather (or felt) soles and lower side of quilted soles. When nearly dry, stick together. Leave overnight to dry thoroughly.

8 If you have made leather soles: After a lot of wear you may like to change the upper part of your scuffs. Immerse the whole scuff in boiling water until the glue softens. Then peel away the leather. Make new upper soles as often as you like.

45